Investing

Strategies For Establishing Passive Income And
Achieving Financial Independence Via Stock Market
Investments, An Exposition On Dividend Stocks And
Achieving Early Retirement

*(An Elementary Blueprint For Commencing Investment
And Embarking On The Journey Towards Financial
Autonomy)*

Jake Lefebvre

TABLE OF CONTENT

Purchasing Single-Family Real Estate

Setting precise financial goals is the first step towards being a successful property finance backer. After two years, five years, ten years, and when you retire, where do you want to be? Do you plan to increase your earnings today in order to focus on your current level of personal fulfillment, or are your venture properties just for your own retirement or the school store for your children? Either way, you can decide what you need to do in order to get out of real estate.

Claiming single-family houses is usually a great way to achieve your goals if you need to save a significant amount of money for retirement or your children's education. If you require income immediately in order to supplement your income and save money for the future, multifamily housing may be a better option for you.

The next step is to carefully consider the level of risk you are willing to accept. Purchasing a home with all of your money is not as risky as purchasing one with profound use. Reducing your influence not only lowers your risks but also lowers your reward. The best method to reduce risk and increase reward is to purchase highly used contracts with positive cash flow while preserving a reserve to help you weather any difficult times down the road. In this part and the ones that follow, I'll walk you through the best approach to take. Please put this book down, get a piece of paper or your computer, and write out your short--, mid-, and long-term goals before moving on.

All of your actions on land should be directed towards achieving these three goals. If the conjecture fails to propel you towards your goals, you should carefully dissect it and redirect your efforts to something that would help you reach your targets. This phase is crucial. Your goals should be written down or printed out and then taped to the mirror.

You should ask yourself, "What will I do today to arrive at those goals?" every morning.

You should ask yourself, "What have I done today to arrive at those goals?" every evening.

If you take responsibility for yourself and adhere to the step-by-step instructions in this book, you will soon achieve freedom from the rat race!

Home Types: Single-family vs. Multifamily

Multifamily homes are a good option if your speculating goals are to generate quick cash and enough of it to allow you to quit your job.

Single-family homes are appropriate for you if you want to purchase properties close to your place of residence so you can carefully inspect them and see them appreciate quickly, building up funds for the future in the process.

Multifamily housing is portrayed as consisting of two to four units. Business multifamily properties are defined as homes with five or more units; I shall discuss these in a later book. The amazing thing about multifamily properties with two to four units is that they can provide a substantial monthly income. They typically prefer a more relaxed lifestyle than single-family houses because the rent you receive determines the majority of their value.

Finding a single-family home that generates positive income is more difficult, even though they often appreciate more quickly than multifamily properties. I'll tell you how to carefully inspect properties to make sure they will provide you with the money you need because I could never advise purchasing a property that doesn't generate income each month.

When you begin your land-contributing enterprise, keep in mind this unbreakable guideline:

Only Invest in Real Estate With Positive Cash Flow!

This is so important that I should emphasize it. The real estate you are buying is an investment. It shouldn't cost you money each month to work or make a claim. Buying a house that requires monthly cash inflow is not a wise decision, just as buying stocks would never require it. Even if you may be working extremely hard right now, what would happen if you lost your job and had a property that you needed to pay an extra $200 or $300 into each month? The property can be lost, or you might have to sell it quickly. You won't always get paid the full value when you have to sell something quickly. Avoid this by carefully reviewing your guesses and only purchasing real estate with a positive cash flow.

Recognize the Market

It's important to ascertain the type of market you're dealing in before entering the home market.

A market where there aren't enough homes available to meet demand is known as a vendors' market. Because there are more buyers than sellers, buyers should compete for houses, which raises prices.

When there is an excess of available homes and a lower number of buyers than sellers, the market is said to be one for buyers. Because retailers have to compete to see customers, prices are reduced. For example, during the Great Recession, there was an incredible buyers' market in several areas because of the massive surplus of houses that were available.

When focusing on your local real estate market, you should truly ask yourself if sellers are in charge of the market and if they have the ability to set prices at nearly any level and receive multiple bids on the same day they list a property. Alternatively, it can be a buyers' market, in which case a good, fairly priced home could be on the market for a very long period, waiting for the right buyer to show up.

It's most likely somewhere in the middle. Perhaps try not to buy if the market is truly a dealers' market. My preference is to buy homes at a discount and resell them for a premium.

Land moves in cycles, so you should talk to your handle and conduct additional research to find out how long the market has been rising and what the general predictions are for the future. Recall that land is a merchant's livelihood, and since they are paid to sell land, they may be overly optimistic. If the market is in favor of buyers, now can be the greatest time to make a purchase. You can find real deals by taking as much time as is necessary. Let it be known that while you can find excellent deals in any market, you should first understand the one you are in.

If the market is one where dealers predominate, you will need to move quickly and make a compelling offer. It's normal to draft a deal by hand under these circumstances and present it to the selling agent as you're looking around the house. This will proceed even further if you hand them a genuine cash cheque and tell them how much you appreciate the property.

In a buyer's market, you can evaluate your options and spend as much time as needed. You have plenty of time, so don't rush into a standard agreement just because you think a deal might close soon. It's likely that your market lies somewhere in the middle of these two boundaries, giving you the chance to make a very informed choice.

Should I Invest Or Pay Off My Debt?

Perhaps the most common question among all first-time investors is this one. I have mentioned the benefits of both up to now. Like the old story about the chicken and the egg, it can seem like a heavy thing to think about when it comes to fulfilling obligations rather than making a contribution. When all is said and done, having fewer obligations will allow you to donate more, and having more contributions will allow you to be paid more to fulfill your obligations. So which strategy is best?

Some people may suggest that you fulfill your obligations before starting to save and make contributions. If you look at the fundamentals, this is sound financial advice. If you are paying fifteen percent on your credit cards, why would you deposit cash into your savings account to obtain a few percent?

This sounds reasonable enough, but in all honesty, this admonition has serious flaws. I can tell you that even if I had waited to contribute and invest money until after all of my bills were paid, I would still be here today. The inclinations that ultimately led to your expenses will persist unless you successfully modify them. Paying off your debts is something you should prioritize in order to raise your FICO score, but you also need to budget for purchases and investments. That being said, there isn't a clear-cut answer, much like the chicken and the egg. Eventually, paying off your debt will improve your FICO score, allowing you to purchase your home at a better interest rate; in the meantime, saving money for real projects is also a wise decision. The most important factor is your approach. Some people have to act immediately before the second disappears. Others can cautiously investigate their path to financial independence. What method works best for you? It's up to you to decide.

Having Cash on Hand Is Essential for Real Estate Investing

When buying real estate, monetary reserves are required. Managed risk is the essence of investing. You are taking a bigger risk than someone with reserves if you start buying properties without them. Investing in real estate can provide challenges. What would happen if you rented to a terrible person who broke everything and didn't pay the rent? You should aspire for the best but prepare for the worst, even though this is not typical.

It is true that having holds might be difficult when you are initially starting out. Regardless of whether it means obtaining an extra Visa or two, submerging them in water, and then storing them in your cooler, you should have some form of backup plan in place. If anything terrible happens, you will truly want to melt the ice and get through the dark period. Additionally, you will have a few hours while the ice melts to be sure you actually need to use the card.

Keep in mind that if you receive a second Visa and don't use it, the available unused credit will help you improve your credit score.

In actuality, you should maintain your stores and quit buying for incentives. If you have the resources to weather these bad times, I assure you that there will be plenty of good times to make up for them.

Understanding Is Strength.

Many people who invest in real estate require your money. A decent arrangement is only one in a thousand strange arrangements, and many liars would be hard-pressed to come up with a better plan than to sell you their fears. This is why you should always conduct your research before purchasing your first property and any subsequent ones.

What would your level of consistency be? You should definitely read publications such as this one and others so you will know exactly what to look for. As you gain experience and establish a reputation, invitations to make appointments will start to come your way. You really want to obtain the info to quickly separate the bad arrangements from the excellent ones because only one out of every odd arrangement is a decent arrangement.

I get excited about five or ten out of every twenty properties that I look at, either financially or truly. I would maybe close on a handful of these after doing more research and make presents on maybe 50% of these. That represents a ratio of one configuration for every ten possible options. This does not include

MLS properties, which are often seen as good values at a discount. You will be successful in land investing if you have the knowledge to quickly identify the misleading advertising, budget summaries, and restorative upgrades that hide the hidden problems.

Even if you don't already have the funds to purchase your first venture property, you should start investigating homes and working on speculating scenarios. You will become an expert in the local real estate market by doing the maths, as I explain in Chapters 4 and 5. When a really good deal presents itself, you'll be able to recognize it quickly and take the right action. It's probably not a decent deal if it seems too good to be true when you first review it. Make use of your senses and have faith in the hard data!

Never make a purchase based just on emotion. I've looked at a tonne of lovely homes that weren't profitable and then turned them down. You will see many amazing configurations available, but it will require patience and self-control.

You will soon be telling your friends about your latest land purchase and the enormous return on investment (ROI) you will receive if you follow the advice in this book. Even though you will eventually move into a nicer home and leave your job, the majority of them won't truly embrace you until then. It requires a lot of effort at first, but when you master the skills, the payoff is huge, and once you're there, you won't need to look back!

Operating Without the Landlord's Approval

Users who operate without their landlords' consent are prohibited by Airbnb as well. Thus, a landlord can suddenly show up and tell you, "Hey, I'm not letting Airbnb in my property." This listing ought not to be on the internet. If Airbnb notices that you frequently rent out homes, list them on the platform without the owner's consent, and receive numerous complaints from landlords, they will deactivate those listings and ban you from the service.

Make sure you and your landlord have formal paperwork before engaging in rental arbitrage. You should be able to service a lease addendum for your landlord stating that they have given you permission to operate your business, should that ever come up.

Not every one of your eggs has to be in one basket. Taking into account the ban, you shouldn't limit your travel to Airbnb. This novel is about Airbnb; I know that now. I reached 100 Airbnb homes. Since it's my social experiment, we're using several platforms. Bookings through Furnish Finder, Copa, and Vrbo come in. Direct reservations and all the benefits. Thus, it would be ideal if you prepared yourself as a knowledgeable and experienced host with experience in multiple properties and across various platforms. Do that simply in case something goes wrong with Airbnb and you are temporarily banned; that way, you still have a distribution channel where your listing can be booked elsewhere while you are appealing to be let back on the platform. Otherwise, it would be perilous for you to go a month without revenue if Airbnb were to close and you were the sole source of bookings.

While it is a terrific place to start, don't limit your business to Airbnb alone. Initially, you can only use Airbnb; subsequently, you can switch to multiple channels. That's what I advise since you have one or two properties when you're tiny, and your representatives clean while you're new. You're not making many reservations, so there isn't a lot of risk exposure.

In the seven years that I have owned properties, I have owned more than one hundred. Despite having made tens of thousands of reservations, we have not been banned from Airbnb. You have a very slim chance of being banned if you take that at face value. However, after your company is formed, you no longer have to assume that risk. Thus, as you're ready, switch to many channels and keep developing and prospering.

Viewers of virtual and augmented reality

The Oculus Rift, created by the same-named firm and later acquired by Facebook, has been much luckier. Since its release in 2016, it has become one of the most well-liked virtual reality game viewers. There are other viewers made by well-known companies to challenge the dominance, and Samsung's Gear VR, which requires the newest smartphone to function and be placed inside the viewer's mask. Additionally, Huawei's

VR2 can be connected to a PC in order to run games meant for computers with more processing power than the integrated one.

Viewer of mixed reality

In the business world, Microsoft's Hololens, a mixed reality viewer that was developed in 2015 and updated in 2019, has, for the time being at least, piqued interest. It is specifically intended to add value to enterprise projects or any work processes that could use some experimentation with new ideas and could benefit from a minimal amount of digital interaction.

Due to the fact that we are discussing the potential and market for augmented and virtual reality today

Increased human powers and freedom from gadgets.

By far, the most information is provided to us by vision: 80–90% of all information that humans get is through vision.

Every mental job we do lowers our ability to complete additional tasks at the same time.

The mental effort needed to process a given sort of information determines the cognitive load. For instance, because words must be understood and letters must be converted into words, reading instructions on a computer screen and following them through raises the cognitive load compared to simply listening to them.

The "cognitive distance," or the difference between the way information is presented and how it is used, also affects the cognitive load.

All of this is made simpler by the sense of sight, which allows us to obtain a vast amount of varied information. almost instantaneously

Because of this, a figure or image that contextualizes the real world for us by superimposing information on it minimizes cognitive burden and reduces cognitive distance. Discusses the effectiveness of AR.

Virtual reality (VR) holds the potential to enable technology to perceive and understand the features of its surroundings, continuously gathering data and taking the place of human senses. This facilitates the interaction between man and his context by enabling the creation of shortcuts.

"Virtual reality frees us from technology because all interactions with the environment take place through natural gestures and no longer through a screen," says Medich. "Today we are slaves dependent on devices."

However, because "they enhance our natural abilities, our sight, our hearing, and our ability to analyze," these technologies also offer a further advantage. Its application domains are therefore essentially infinite."

Growth market leading the way in AR.

Between now and 2023, the worldwide VR and AR market is projected to increase at a rate of 58.1%, having peaked at $6.158 billion in 2017. The market for connectivity and information technology will be driven by the increasing use of smartphones and technological advancements, as well as by the large investments and inventions made by tech behemoths like Apple, Google, and Facebook in the form of tools, platforms, and services.

About 60% of the overall turnover is accounted for by virtual reality, but by 2023, the ratio should be reversed: AR will grow at a pace greater than virtual reality, at 73.8%. AR is supposed to be driven by consumer demand in industries like tourism and retail. This will contribute to a market that is expected to reach $215 billion in the next two to three years.

An analogous argument may be made about the hardware-software divide: currently, hardware devices, such as virtual reality viewers, account for around 65% of the sector's turnover. However, the need for software solutions is expected to grow at a quicker rate and become closer to these percentages. Even while Canada, Central Eastern Europe, and Western Europe will see faster rates of development than the USA, which currently leads this new market, is predicted to hold its top spot for the next four years.

Although researchers have projected market growth by combining virtual reality with augmented reality, developers are adamant that augmented reality will be the primary driver of growth in the next years. According to Digital Trends, "augmented reality (AR) understands and includes the real world, whereas virtual reality (VR) reproduces the real world to create digital spaces. AR superimposes virtual images on real environments, spaces, and images, creating a potential for customer experiences that are very different from those possible with VR."

VR environments aren't suitable for actual social contact outside of a digital world since they demand the whole attention of the user (who is submerged in a completely recreated environment in which he can move and interact only "digitally").

Rather, augmented reality (AR) makes it possible—and this is exactly where its power resides—by acting as a "co-pilot" on-demand in daily life and seamlessly blending into users' regular interactions with the outside world.

Interactions that can occur in business and job settings, as well as in gaming, entertainment, sports, and shopping environments: According to 64% of American customers, augmented reality will even improve the workplace by speeding up the design and innovation processes or making it easier for teams in different places to collaborate.

82% of businesses that are now using these solutions think the benefits are greater than they anticipated, 46% of respondents think AR and VR will become commonplace in the next three years, and 38% think it will happen in the next three to five years.

Because it can interact with reality, augmented reality is generally thought to be more practical in the workplace. However, certain virtual reality solutions are also thought to have the potential to have a good effect on businesses.

While 36% of businesses employ virtual reality, 45% of businesses use augmented reality (AR); the remaining businesses are still in the experimental stage.

PREVISION

Predictions about cryptocurrencies must begin with their origins, which are not all that old! Actually, the cryptocurrency industry began in 2009 when Satoshi Nakamoto released Bitcoin (BTC), the greatest cryptocurrency with the highest market capitalization, onto the market.

Eleven years later, cryptographic currencies have surpassed the 5,000 computerized monetary standards on CoinMarketCap, making them an incredibly amazing part of contemporary culture.

Forecasts on digital currencies are essential for differentiating between those that can lead us to lose our investment funds, those that can make us buy in search of the best return on speculation (ROI), and—worse yet—those virtual monetary standards that are merely tricks. Forecasts of the value of digital currencies are therefore essential for determining which cryptographic currencies to invest in in 2021.

Before moving on to our section about expectations for digital money, let us point out that the financial business sectors are currently experiencing complete surprise as a result of the COVID-19 pandemic, which has wreaked havoc on stock markets.

Going back to the business sectors, you don't have to be an expert to understand how much volatility affects their tools.

As an example, we ought to analyze the Bitcoin trend for the year that just ended, specifically 2020. The year began with the cryptocurrency that was the most valuable in the world, costing over seven thousand dollars.

Following the start of the pandemic, it dropped precipitously, hitting 4,900. However, from that point on, there has been a steady increase that reached above $19,000 in October. By December 2020, the value of a Bitcoin had increased to over $15,000 USD, with an annual growth rate of + 156%.

But at the beginning of 2021, this particular coin performed better than expected, reaching 30,000 dollars—as we mentioned at the beginning of the section—and earning a 302% increase!

All things considered, 2020 seems to have been a significant year for digital currencies, especially when we consider the impact of Bitcoin. However, 2019 is also looking incredibly promising. Another important factor is the notable partnerships that Bitcoin has established with the industry leader in payments, Visa, and the blockchain startup Fold to provide a Visa that will allow customers to be reimbursed in Bitcoin for their typically large purchases. Companies and platforms such as Nike (NKE), Airbnb, Amazon (AMZN), Uber, etc. It is obvious that the goal of this action was to increase daily Bitcoin usage as much as possible.

Virtual money indices are created annually; therefore, in order to predict what lies ahead in 2021, it would be wiser to start by analyzing the state of digital currencies as of right now and analyzing their trends for the year that is about to end. This follows a very successful 2019 in which interest in cryptocurrencies has increased significantly in comparison to earlier in the year.

Even though cryptocurrency has made amazing returns in 2020, some have outperformed others, and this bull market is expected to continue into 2021.

Strong and Lucrative Learning Instructions

(1) Before lending money on real estate, always check the title and obtain a moneylender's title protection plan. (2) Before lending money on real estate,

make sure you fully understand all the terms of the arrangement, including the worth, the amount of work required for remodeling, and the financial circumstances.

(3) Before you lend money, confirm what the borrower says.

(4) Before funding the deal, get legal counsel to make sure you didn't overlook anything that would have made your speculation vulnerable.

It Pours When It Rains

Kurt's organization failed, which resulted in his layoff, and on top of that, the retirement benefits he had been counting on vanished, too. Anyway, unlike many of his more seasoned partners, he truly had the chance to manage his retirement account in the future. Once he found another job, he took charge of his situation and began learning about land investment instead of relying on an institution for his long-term financial security.

Kurt came up with a plan that involved leasing newly built homes that were financed over an extended period of time. His goal was to have six houses claimed free of charge (without a house loan) by the time he retired, and the rental income would serve as his retirement income. Kurt had to keep his property and the executives simple by owning all of the units in a similar region, as opposed to diversifying his portfolio across different regions. Kurt then ended up purchasing six brand-new residences in a newly developed area over the course of two years.

He had his ups and downs with tenants, just like any other property manager, but he managed to complete the job by refusing to sell any of his properties, even though he was very tempted to do so on a few occasions. In the end, he had completely paid off all six house loans and reached his retirement target.

It was around that time that a late-spring evening tempest with lightning and heavy rain arrived. But this storm lingered for several days, longer than any previous rainstorm that anyone could remember. Furthermore, the heavy rains continued. After four days, the low-lying areas began to fill with water, and the primary signs of flooding became apparent.

Although they could see what was happening, meteorologists were unable to explain why, to the best of their knowledge, this intense downpour storm would not move eastward like previous tempests had. Numerous homes began to experience water in their unfinished basements and plumbing spaces, and the long-term flood zone regions shown on FEMA maps began to flood.

But they failed to account for a phenomenon like this storm. Ultimately, the water level surpassed the dam's height, causing water to overflow and considerably increasing the volume of the typically overflowing stream on the dam's opposite side. Everyone living downstream of the dam was warned by the news to flee because a dam failure could have disastrous consequences.

The homes Kurt purchased for his retirement were situated in a development downstream of that dam. His properties were still near the waterway that was currently overflowing due to the excessive water rushing over the dam, even though they were not in a flood zone. His occupants had safely evacuated, leaving him with no choice but to stay glued to the news and observe the events transpire.

When the rain stopped, the dam held together, and the rising waters began to settle, he thought he had luck. He rushed over to see how high the water rose precisely when the streets in that area were secure. It was more unfortunate than he had thought. Every one of his properties had the second floor covered with water. They should be demolished since they were completely destroyed.

Since flood damage was prohibited by his peril protection strategy, he was not eligible for any assistance from the property protection he had been dependable in paying for for over 16 years. Many property owners were assisted by the federal government organization FEMA when their home insurance company refused to pay claims. Kurt, however, received no help from them because investment properties were not eligible for relief.

He evaluated his options, listed his now six empty parts for sale, and eventually sold them for almost nothing.

This incredibly depressing tale teaches some incredibly important lessons.

Strong and Lucrative Learning Instructions

(1) Even in areas that are not in a flood zone, floods can occur. To be honest, a lot of people don't realize how common flooding is near lakes, rivers, and oceans. In this sense, if you own properties near water or in other low-lying areas, you

should definitely think about purchasing flood protection.

(2) Spread out the properties you rent out. Even though claiming in a similar region makes sense for a variety of reasons (laws, neighborhood, group dynamics, etc.), gathering all of your properties in one location can lead to complications. For example, a tornado or a flood typically affects some areas of a place more than others. Spreading out your property over different parts of a region can help protect you from catastrophic events that would destroy everything you own. Additionally, some neighborhoods improve more than others, especially over the long term, and sometimes this is hard to predict. What is a prosperous area now might be a bad area of town tomorrow. And, years

later, a place that now seems like a minimal area might turn out to be the most desirable and hot place to live.

Applying My Cycling Experience To Manage Market Volatility

Because of this week's market volatility, some of you are feeling uneasy. Because you have been trained to deal with volatility and profit from the markets, some of you are beaming with pride. Regardless of your stance, I think we can all benefit from this lesson I learned from riding bikes when it comes to investing.

Have you seen the riders in the Tour de France (TDF) on television as they maneuver through hairpin turns and downslopes at speeds of up to 100 kph at certain points before stopping and restarting the descent? While terrifying, it also makes your heart race, doesn't it?

Although I missed the opportunity to ride on one of the most well-known TDF stages, Alped'Huez, I did get to ride in Taiwan back in 2017.

I had the opportunity to descend Yang Ming Shan, a 30-minute descent, back then, even though there weren't many long, winding downslopes in Singapore.

When I was climbing the mountain, I was astounded by how quickly the local riders descended the slope. How were they able to accomplish that?

In response to my inquiry about the trick, my local guide grinned and said, "It is not as hard as it seems, I will tell you later when we reach the top." I ascended for almost an hour before reaching the summit and relaxing. The tour guide stated: "Paul, when you descend later, I want you to look 10–15 metres ahead when you negotiate the bends." I thought, Why already? I want to look directly in front of me because I am more worried about the sharp turns! The guide motioned for me to follow him down the slope without much warning, so I did.

I was breaking like crazy on the first few slopes. As I got closer to a bend, I could feel myself making a concerted effort to slow down. However, I saw my guide quickly back off, and as we descended the mountain, he quickly vanished from view. When I navigated the bends at 5 meters, 7 meters, and finally 10 meters, I decided to look farther after recalling his words with a certain amount of blind faith.

I noticed that it was much easier now, that the bend didn't appear to be as steep, and that I could descend much faster. With this newfound self-assurance, I simply continued to look ahead further down the road, seeing the turn-off each time, and my body naturally swayed and adjusted as needed.

What is the story's lesson, and how does it apply to investing? Sometimes, in investing, it's necessary to look beyond the immediate fluctuations and focus on longer-term trends. If you had attempted to trade the market every day for the past two weeks since March 9, you would have realized that it has essentially been one day up and one day down every time.

On the other hand, it is immediately apparent from the chart that there is a downward trend.

Consequently, we always advise you to trade the trend (longer term) in Ultimate Investing. As long as you are aware of the general direction of the longer trend, it doesn't matter if you are unable to catch every wave or the short-term daily movements.

I hope you find this nugget of wisdom useful. Please write the phrase "TRADE WISE, TRADE SAFELY" on this page if you enjoyed what you read.

You Get To Pick Your Coworkers

It is best to collaborate with others in almost all typical work environments. Usually, you don't have a lot of influence over who those people are.

It's likely that you will have to put up with someone you don't like, be forced to attend staff meetings with that one jerk-off you constantly detest, and there's a good chance you won't get along with your desk neighbor. There are countless circumstances where you won't feel the same way about one of your partners. You also genuinely have no control over who comes and goes.

49

If you are a financial backer of land, things are entirely different. You are the owner and manager of your own wisdom as a financial backer. You get to make the decisions, organize your work however you see fit, decide how to complete tasks and create your own schedule. You also get to choose who you collaborate with. You have more freedom to select your coworkers here than in a cubicle, and you're not required to work with the same people every day. It's a very fluid environment, and you don't have to collaborate with someone you detest. When you find good people that you enjoy working with, you can then make an effort to maintain them on your team and build as strong of a relationship as possible. Ultimately, the choice is always yours.

The fact remains, though, that land contribution is also a highly character-filled industry (to put it nicely). Even though you have the freedom to choose who you collaborate with and don't collaborate with, there are situations when the ideal person is merely a butt sphincter for a particular task or administration. There are no rules about how someone must behave or what kind of character they must possess when contributing land.

It's even plausible that at least one of your so-called "associates" has engaged in criminal activity at some point in the past. In one way or another, that's just part of the work. Not that I encounter a lot of murderers in the land, but I have worked with a lot of people who have found themselves in a tight spot at some point because of something related to land, numbers, money, or who knows what else. The reasoning for this, in my opinion, is twofold: first, there are so many vague scenarios in the land that it's easy to unintentionally find yourself in one and cause issues; second, contributing land can attract particular character traits. Think about it: formal training isn't necessary, client support isn't necessary, creativity is needed, and danger is always implied. Many criminals fell neatly into those categories and skill levels. Moreover, there is no requirement for individual verifications when contributing land, which benefits the less honorable individuals.

Positively, real estate investing is the ideal choice if you've always wanted to work in a field full of interesting people! The fact that you can choose who you work with and who you don't work with within this industry is still relevant. I don't know of any other profession that allows for such flexibility unless you are an entrepreneur.

An Opportunity to Show Some Backbone

It's safe to say that in this field, having a backbone will be necessary to combat the not-so-unexpected lack of customer service. In this industry, people move quickly and hard, leaving little time for spoilers. This is more of a problem than people essentially intending evil with their disturbing characters. Furthermore, it's not necessary to concentrate on the experience; contributing is and always will be about the numbers. Modern financial backers will typically be exposed for their mistaken belief that experience counts when it really should only be about the numbers. When people realize that everything truly comes down to the numbers, that's what they really care about, and the customer service and experience aspects can easily come second.

Utilizing your spine may not always be welcomed if you work a 9–5 job. Actually, you might actually gain some enemies from it. On the other hand, one needs a spine when contributing land. It might never come in handy, but just in case, it should be kept as a backup. Sometimes, bad things happen, and in those situations, you have to be

52

ready to enact laws. If you're not prepared to do that, someone can take advantage of you and your money right away.

Using your spine simply means you don't let people run over you; it doesn't in the slightest require you to yell or lose it at anyone. When necessary, you assert your authority, make sure the necessary things happen, and then you move on.

Contributing land won't be for you if you are hesitant and prefer to stick to yourself. Many people never have to speak up, depending on how they choose to participate, but you almost always need to protect your project. Furthermore, even if you never have to use your back, you should still exercise initiative.

Determine the Type of Property That's Ideal for You

Remain in Your Lane

This is something I have said before and will continue to say. With Lifestyle Assets, there is no one-size-fits-all solution. That is what is so amazing about them. It's not necessary to locate a tiny, hard-to-find object in order to succeed. In almost every market, there are plenty of opportunities.

The best choice for you will depend on your situation and goals, but here are some suggestions. Assets related to way of life differ greatly from traditional land ventures. There are gaps everywhere. The most astounding feature? It isn't brain surgery.

Generally, I advise people to "stay in your path." To put it another way, look for homes that you might want to stay in and areas that you enjoy visiting, and I'll show you how to locate valuable lifestyle assets there.

Don't be complicated! To begin, consider what kind of property most appeals to you.

Don't make this too complicated. When putting together your portfolio, there are a lot of decisions you can make, and all of them have to do with your lifestyle and the financial goals we looked at earlier in this book. I've spent about 19 years assisting financial backers in finding properties, and I often make things too complicated. I've expended a lot of effort looking for fix-and-flip properties, advancement deals, and multi-family deals that will generate cash. Those kinds of land deals, in my opinion, are much more akin to finding a needle in a haystack.

I first spent a lot of time and effort creating elaborate calculations and accounting pages in Excel. I assembled multiple approximations and extracted data from diverse analysis sources. Everything I was told indicated that there isn't a single extraordinary type of property, nor is there a single exceptional area that seems preferable to others. Keep it simple at first because there are so many options in this area. Again, it will depend more on your preferences and needs than on the kind of property and its location. You do need to double-check everything at the same time with the sources of information I mentioned later, but ultimately, the decision rests with you until further notice.

Now, let's get started. First of all, what kind of property do you cherish the most? Most people have a preference based on the area they have chosen. Sometimes, it's an indisputable choice and the most prevalent kind of property in the area, but it doesn't have to be. Let me explain. A more understated townhouse or loft-style apartment suite in the heart of the action is a noticeable choice in a particularly urban area, but there might also be some amazing opportunities outside of it. Occasionally, the most advantageous properties are also the most common because the majority of people visit and stay in those types of properties. Occasionally, though, you will notice amazing liberties with the subtler property types in a space. To find those opportunities, you should be aware of where to find the information.

Depending on the different areas I have chosen to invest in, I have different tendencies. If I purchase in an area where there is a lot going on, I need my guests to be close to the activity. Therefore, I purchase properties that have more of a hotel feel, right in the middle of the action and close to the attractions. Reasonably assembled apartment suites or condos are usually easy to locate. Reason-assembled networks that are made to look like retreats can be seen in many resort towns. With amenities akin to those of a resort, they are equipped for daily rentals. I enjoy those kinds of properties because they give guests the impression that they are at a resort.

As for the drawbacks of those kinds of properties, we talked about the fact that you will compete directly with the retreats and somewhat more directly with the lodgings. These thoughtfully designed townhomes and apartments have certain advantages and disadvantages, but the resorts will provide slightly more competition.

On the other hand, I tend to favor single-family homes that are more tranquil or private if I purchase a region that is more of an escape or goal, whether it be a nature objective, a sentimental escape, an open-air insight, or any combination of those things. I also really enjoy the unique properties, such as tree houses, RVs, tiny bungalows, and yurts—those quirky, entertaining properties that enable us to provide our guests with an absolutely remarkable experience. As you can see, depending on different areas, I have different inclinations.

The Niches Hold the Riches

You have probably heard the saying "wealth is in the specialties" if you have ever prepared for a showcase. This will be covered in great detail when we discuss how to set up and market your property to attract the best buyer. Right now, you should consider who your ideal guests should be and make sure the kind of property you choose will appeal to them.

I'm not going to look at four-, five-, or six-room houses if I need to entice and arrange a sentimental getaway for couples. I will check out this cozy, fun, and private two-room bungalow where a couple can have a peaceful, heartfelt getaway. I won't look for the tiny houses if my primary interest group is families. I need the guardians, kids, and possibly multiple families or generations to get together in some of these areas where family get-togethers are not something to laugh at. I'm not going to look for a minimalist house or yurt. I'll look for the larger nearby homes. I'll look for larger single-family homes with separate living quarters and plenty of space for everyone to use as a base of operations. By making sure the property type requests to the gathering that you're adjusting, that's what I mean. You should first consider who your ideal client is, and then you will provide the appropriate property to support that ideal client.

The best short-term rental hosts in any area don't try to please everyone. They are incredibly intelligent, and, more importantly, very clear about who their ideal interest group is and isn't. You have to be very astute when identifying your primary interest group. You will also repel people you don't need with that property if you are very clear about who you need to attract and purchase a type of property that fits their needs.

Stay on your path when choosing your ideal interest group. You should be with the people in your interest group. Once you are part of the right interest group, choosing, setting up, and advertising real estate will be easy because you are familiar with them and can communicate in their language.

Trading in Swings

A swing trader finds daily fluctuations in stocks, commodities, and currencies. A swing trade may take several weeks to turn a profit, in contrast to day trading. When it comes to their trade opening, swing traders are more tenacious. Although there are generally fewer trading opens, as the positions extend to the second day, there is the potential for enormous benefits on a single trade. Anyone with the necessary funds and expertise to invest can try their hand at swing trading.

Swing Trading progressively focuses research and information on macroeconomics and calls for fewer technical investigative skills. Since the moves that swing traders are anticipating are larger, the entry focus and planning don't need to be as precise.

The trader doesn't have to invest a lot of time in swing trading because regular technical analysis and regular screen time are not required. Generally, it's a low-stress, low-effort job. Since the swing trader is not required to spend his entire day staring at a computer screen, he is able to work a second full-time job.

Typically, swing traders need time to practice. The likelihood of making more money from a trade than from trading the same security several times a day increases with the length of time the trade is open, either in days or weeks. Swing trades require larger margin requirements because positions are held overnight. Swing trading leverage is typically two times the trader's capital, as opposed to day trading, which has a maximum leverage of four times one's capital.

Stop-losses and target levels are important concepts for day traders to grasp and apply to their advantage. Even though there's a chance the stop order will execute at a disadvantage, it's still preferable to constantly keep an eye on all of your open positions.

Swing traders can lose money, as is typical with all forms of trading, and since they hold their positions for a longer period of time, they might lose more money than day traders.

Using cutting-edge technology is not necessary for swing trading. With just one computer and any required trading tools, swing trading is possible.

Since swing trading is typically not a full-time job, swing traders have other sources of income and are less likely to experience stress-related burnout.

When is the best time to start day trading?

The following highlights the perfect circumstances for you to become a day trader:

You have a strong will, discipline, and diligence.

You accept the possibility of making modest daily gains from modest trades.

If and when they apply to you, you have the minimum capital requirements specified by SEC and FINRA rules for pattern day traders.

You possess the know-how and proficiency to generate substantial earnings.

You have the ability to handle stress and are not easily stressed.

You are constantly seeking excitement and never have a boring day.

When is the right time to start swing trading?

The following highlights the perfect circumstances for you to become a swing trader:

You don't know a great deal about technical matters.

You don't want to pursue trading as a full-time career. In other words, you don't want trading to be your sole source of revenue.

You will choose something less hazardous than day trading because you dislike stress.

You're not into continuously keeping an eye on market activity.

You have the patience to watch the market's movements for weeks or months.

You can't find time for day trading because you work a full-time job.

You don't have a lot of money to put down.

Where Are Buyers Supposed to Be?

It would be better to label this section. How do my clients find me? People who truly value and could gain from your services will eventually come across you. You need to have multiple backup sources in case one of your current sources of qualified leads runs out, so you should be actively networking and promoting to attract new ones.

We'll be concentrating primarily on the rehab/investor buyer here.

We'll talk about owner/occupied retail purchaser options later, but for now, let's concentrate on your primary source—the person who can recognize a fantastic investment opportunity and close swiftly.

When you first start out, you might want to run the advertisement for two or three weeks straight to start building your base. Later, you might want to cut back to once a month to maintain opportunities and fresh resources.

Several inexpensive advertisements might put you well on your way to assembling a strong buyer list. As you add and remove prospects over time, your buyer's list should grow. Dealing with clients means you will inevitably encounter some, let's say, dishonest people.

Individuals that wish to take advantage of you, possibly by attempting to wholesale your wholesale agreement (which wouldn't be so bad if they actually completed the deal).

Customers will want you to tell them about your deals or the location of the property when you first start accepting calls from advertising, and you are fresh new with no inventory of homes to sell. You are not required to avoid the matter. Just say you're a hard worker who prefers great bids to little ones and that you just need some serious buyers at this point. Being entirely honest with the individual you are chatting with, telling them that you mostly deal in wholesale-grade deals, and asking them to call them again once you have a home under contract is absolutely in your best interests.

Regardless of where they came from, when a potential buyer reacts to your advertisement, ask them the questions you just read about in the What You Need to Know section.

Based on their answers, you will be able to categorize them as either strong, prospective or somewhat possible prospects.

Recall that you shouldn't disregard them just because they don't have excellent credit or haven't bought 100 homes. For some of those folks, you will be their bank in the future.

Talking about how much earnest money they would consider putting down now would be putting the wagon before the horse. In reality, when answering these questions, some of the participants can be cautious or even evasive. To ascertain if a buyer is sincere, ask them any of these questions informally. Most sincere and morally-minded buyers won't mind answering.

When speaking with the prospect, keep your tone casual and conversational. An "I'm here to assist" demeanor is ideal, and the questions you pose shouldn't sound like they belong on a telemarketing survey. You'll be depending on these folks for your paychecks. Therefore, it would be beneficial to familiarise yourself with their styles of buying and margins.

Asking the last question on the list, "Do you have a bank qualifying letter that you could provide me for the correct sort of deal?" may be a little bold, but it can help you identify the people who are genuinely driven right away. Regardless of whether they have a bank letter or not, you will do business with some quite capable buyers. On the other hand, a person who goes to the trouble of producing a bank letter stating that Mrs. Johnson is a pre-approved customer for real estate transactions is highly significant.

This quickly sets you apart from the kind of buyers you're looking for—those who take business as seriously as you do. The caliber of the eligible purchasers is more important to you than building a big network of contacts.

Maintain a record of every prospect you speak with, making note of all the relevant details from your fact-finding interview, including contact details like name, home phone number, cell phone number, fax number, and email address.

You have to keep them on file even if some of them don't seem to be noteworthy. Some of the offers you receive will seem extremely low, but you can make these deals work provided you have a contract with a motivated seller who gives you no-risk terms to proceed. You can design your marketing effort so that even transactions or buyers you consider to be marginal can turn into profitable ventures.

You can gain some customers just by giving them a call, and this is a terrific way to establish new business connections. Simply putting your name out there while marketing to find buyers for offers helps people to associate you with great deals, and then the money and buyers usually find their way to you. Many calls will come in stating something like, "I'm a friend of John Doe, and he told me you sell properties." Please include me on your buyer's list. Once you get going, creating a strong buyers list is actually not that hard; all you have to do is keep making adjustments to it as you

go.

Several inexpensive advertisements might put you well on your way to assembling a strong buyer list. As you add and remove prospects over time, your buyer's list should grow. Dealing with clients means you will inevitably encounter some, let's say, dishonest people.

Individuals that wish to take advantage of you, possibly by attempting to wholesale your wholesale agreement (which wouldn't be so bad if they actually completed the deal).

Customers will want you to tell them about your deals or the location of the property when you first start accepting calls from advertising, and you are fresh new with no inventory of homes to sell. You are not required to avoid the matter. Just say you're a hard worker who prefers great bids to little ones and that you just need some serious buyers at this point. Being entirely honest with the individual you are chatting with, telling them that you mostly deal in wholesale-grade deals, and asking them to call them again once you have a home under contract is absolutely in your best interests.

Regardless of where they came from, when a potential buyer reacts to your advertisement, ask them the questions you just read about in the What You Need to Know section.

Based on their answers, you will be able to categorize them as either strong, prospective or somewhat possible prospects.

Recall that you shouldn't disregard them just because they don't have excellent credit or haven't bought 100 homes. For some of those folks, you will be their bank in the future.

Talking about how much earnest money they would consider putting down now would be putting the waggon before the horse. In reality, when answering these questions, some of the participants can be cautious or even evasive. To ascertain if a buyer is sincere, ask them any of these questions informally. Most sincere and morally-minded buyers won't mind answering.

When speaking with the prospect, keep your tone casual and conversational. An "I'm here to assist" demeanour is ideal, and the questions you pose shouldn't sound like they belong on a telemarketing survey. You'll be depending on these folks for your paychecks. Therefore, it would be beneficial to familiarise yourself with their styles of buying and margins.

Asking the last question on the list, "Do you have a bank qualifying letter that you could provide me for the correct sort of deal?" may be a little bold, but it can help you identify the people who are genuinely driven right away. Regardless of whether they have a bank letter or not, you will do business with some quite capable buyers. On the other hand, a person who goes to the trouble of producing a bank letter stating that Mrs. Johnson is a pre-approved customer for real estate transactions is highly significant.

This quickly sets you apart from the kind of buyers you're looking for—those who take business as seriously as you do. The calibre of the eligible purchasers is more important to you than building a big network of contacts.

Maintain a record of every prospect you speak with, making note of all the relevant details from your fact-finding interview, including contact details like name, home phone number, cell phone number, fax number, and email address. You have to keep them on file even if some of them don't seem to be noteworthy. Some of the offers you receive will seem extremely low, but you can make these deals work provided you have a contract with a motivated seller who gives you no-risk terms to proceed. You can design your marketing effort so that even transactions or buyers you consider to be marginal can turn into profitable ventures.

You can gain some customers just by giving them a call, and this is a terrific way to establish new business connections. Simply putting your name out there while marketing to find buyers for offers helps people to associate you with great deals, and then the money and buyers usually find their way to you. Many calls will come in stating something like, "I'm a friend of John Doe, and he told me you sell properties." Please include me on your buyer's list. Once you get going, creating a strong buyers list is actually not that hard; all you have to do is keep making adjustments to it as you do.

The Young Man Who Desired
Independent Employment

Jason resembled Ralph quite a bit. He struggled academically and had no idea what his interest was or what would be the best thing to do. He also lacked a clear goal or purpose. He was aware that he intended to amass fortune rather than work for anybody else. He made the decision to enroll in his university's business school with the goal of starting his own company as soon as he finished.

Working as a desk clerk and porter at a hotel, Jason met the owner, who also owned two other hotels close to the school, and together they made a good living. Jason was employed at the one he worked at. At any time of day or night, visitors could purchase cookies, chips, candies, and refreshments from vending machines at the other hotels. The owner trusted Jason and liked him. Jason was tasked with keeping his three properties' vending machines in working order. Jason had a lot of money to manage as a result. The machines had to be loaded, and the cash had to be emptied afterward. He gained extensive knowledge of the vending machine sector.

As graduation drew close, Jason, a senior, started searching for a company to buy. He looked for "Business Opportunities" in the local newspaper's classified advertising. This occurred much before the Internet. One day, he stumbled upon a vending machine route that was for sale. After haggling with the owner, he was able to buy the truck and thirty machines.

As a fresh college graduate, Jason drove to fill beer, cigarette, and candy machines every day. It took around twenty hours a week to fill them, but that wasn't all. His sole responsibility was to load and repair the machinery. This was frequently challenging.

When Jason returned, he had to count the money and put the coins in coin wrappers. In order to order goods, complete the necessary papers, load the truck, and accept delivery, he had to get to the bank. He didn't have the time or energy to make many sales calls, but he still wanted to expand his company. He would need to install a machine when he eventually obtained a new account. There was only one individual who could complete this difficult mission. He made the decision to give a pal a call and ask for assistance setting one up. It was laborious and time-consuming for him. He soon came to the conclusion that in order to add staff, he needed to grow his company.

After searching for a different vending company to buy for a few hours, he eventually located one after nine months. Jason didn't have much money, but he was able to arrange a payment plan because the seller was motivated to sell his company. Jason managed to merge his previous route with the newly created one. The individual proved to be a wonderful help and an excellent seller, having an understanding of vending machines. Jason quickly acquired two more vending machines by employing the same low-down payment strategy. In the end, he owned a sizable company with several workers.

Looking back, Jason acknowledges that he no longer enjoys managing companies. He continued searching for business opportunities because he enjoyed finding and negotiating agreements. He saw in the newspaper's "Business Opportunity" section a telephone answering service that was for sale.

In his words, "Telephones."Technology.Electronics. Electronics appeal to me.

Why not? Despite the company's dire financial situation, he bought it. This verified the previously provided information. A person will frequently agree to a deal if they are attempting to sell their firm.

Before long, Jason discovered another phone answering service that was losing money. He purchased the business and integrated it with paging, cell phones, which were just being released, and voicemail—which at the time was still a new technology—in order to reduce overhead. Each sculpture was huge and cost $2,000 apiece. The owner's vehicle's trunk had to hold the operating parts.

The business offered more than just answering services. It was a fully operational telecom business that was gaining ground swiftly. Now, he was spending less time at the vending machine business with Jason, his first employee. He kept looking for telecom businesses to buy for the least amount of money.

The telecommunications sector was challenging and stressful at the time despite its popularity. Employees had to work seven days a week, twenty-four hours a day. At three in the morning, Jason would get a call from the company informing him that the computer system was down. This indicated that not all of the clients—including physicians, attorneys, and business owners—had functioning phones. As soon as he could, he would get out of bed and dash to the office to reset the system. He was too busy managing his company to realize how challenging it was despite the fact that it was quite stressful.

After five or six years, Jason received an approach from a representative of a corporation in a city 100 miles away who wanted to buy the business. Although Jason had no intention of selling, he decided to accept the generous offer.

Jason had not considered selling his company before to it. He didn't buy the companies to sell; instead, he bought them to run and profit from. That encounter taught him something important. Being on the receiving end of a sale is a thrilling experience. He had built something with a lot of effort and sold it. When Jason was heading back to the city where the agreement had been finalized, he recalls making a stop at a restaurant. He was sitting at a booth with his bill in hand, completely overcome with joy. Pavlov, the dog, went through the dopamine-releasing process of starting, purchasing, and selling a business. He says purchasing one can liberate a lot of money but also lead to worry, anxiety, and tension. This is two wins in one. When you sell, you can get rid of all of your worries and receive a lot more money. There are two bonuses here. It's twofold advantageous. You are no longer required to be a company prisoner. Being worry- and anxiety-free is such a relief. Jason started searching for other companies that he could purchase, develop, or launch.

There is much caution in this story. Jason founded and sold a number of companies. He amassed enormous wealth. At this point, Jason's net worth might be in the hundreds of millions or even over a billion dollars. There was a moment when he nearly lost everything.

He had four enterprises at the time, all of which were cross-leveraged. His four enterprises were collateral for a large loan he owed to a bank. That was the start of the recession. Sales dropped off fast. He was losing a lot of money and was having trouble making his loan installments. Jason's attorney suggested that he file for Chapter Eleven bankruptcy. Jason wished for nothing to come to pass. Jason avoided going bankrupt by successfully negotiating a restructuring of the firms with the bank. He acknowledged having a nervous breakdown and vowed never to repeat the same mistake. He wouldn't have taken as many chances and wouldn't have borrowed as much money.

He would have exercised greater caution when selecting the companies to acquire. The "High Energy, Low Margin" category is covered in Chapter 2. These two people lost the most money during the recession. Jason declares he won't make any more investments in companies falling within this category. He currently only searches for, acquires, or launches companies in the "Low Energy, HighMargin" sector.

My tolerance for risk is moderate. Which investing techniques are best for me?

Having a medium risk appetite has the advantage of allowing you to incorporate high-risk components into your plan. Having a moderate risk tolerance means you'll never miss out on interesting opportunities. However, you will also balance the possible large winners with low-risk investments that yield less thrilling returns in order to make sure you don't go bankrupt.

The drawback of having a medium-risk profile is that you won't likely make a lot of money in a few weeks. It is imperative that you consider intervals of six months. You should ideally be ready to keep onto shares for a long time. Renowned investor Philip Fisher notably owned Motorola stock from 1955 until his passing in 2004.

The ideal approach to investing with medium risk is to build a diverse portfolio.

What Constitutes A Diversified Portfolio's Fundamental Balance?

Start with a straightforward allocation of 40% bonds and 60% stocks.

Why is the balance between bonds and stocks in a diversified portfolio this way? Because bonds typically appreciate in value when the value of stocks declines. This is because people view them as secure havens, which makes them more well-liked and causes their value to climb.

To achieve a more conservatively diversified portfolio, consider allocating 40% of your portfolio to stocks and 60% to bonds. Recall that investing in funds (such as ETFs) that simultaneously invest in multiple companies or bonds or entire markets (through indexes) is a great method to tighten up your risk management. Money distributes risk. In particular, exchange-traded funds (ETFs) have gained a lot of traction due to their excellent risk distribution and inexpensive fees when compared to conventional mutual funds. For example, the SPDR S&P 500 Trust ETF is a wonderful addition to any diversified portfolio because it tracks the index of the whole stock market.

What further investments should I make for my well-rounded portfolio?

Consider adding one greater risk item to your portfolio at the same time as you add one lower risk asset to maintain balance.

Thus, for instance, if you would like to allocate 1% -5 % of your portfolio to cryptocurrency, make sure that 1% -5 % is also allocated to a low-risk asset. Gold is a fantastic, low-risk investment. Although the price of gold rarely soars, it has done so during the 2007–2008 financial crisis, rising by more than four times. Since gold is a commodity that people will always desire to buy, investors often purchase it during difficult times in the stock market.

My appetite for risk is modest. Which investing techniques are best for me?

In the financial markets, a diversified low-risk portfolio would be well-founded on a combination of bonds, index funds, and blue-chip equities.

If you're looking for low-risk investing outside of the financial markets, consider bank retail products.

Annuities are a prime illustration of a low-risk financial instrument. A common pension product for retirement planning is an annuity. In exchange for a succession of payments over time, you pay a lump sum upfront under this arrangement.

You will get more money than you invested if you persevere and the issuing company does not fail. The issue with annuities is that you don't get very good interest rates. If you find yourself struggling to keep up with inflation, annuities salespeople will likely argue otherwise!

A retail bank high-interest savings account is among the least risky financial investment products. Even if you truly can't afford to lose money, give this a go. However, once more, be sure that the interest rates being offered are more than the rate of inflation. If not, your money will lose value over time while it sits there.

How can I determine which stocks are best for me?

In general, you should search for stocks with increasing value.

Alternatively, you might hunt for equities you believe will lose value and "go short" on them. This entails purchasing them through a specific arrangement with your broker so that you profit when they decline. In a bear market, when prices are generally declining, this can be a useful strategy, but only if you are trading short-term. Furthermore, trading is not the ideal technique for a novice to accumulate riches over time.

SELECTION OF STOCK

Selecting the appropriate stocks for your portfolio is known as stock picking. There are numerous methods for accomplishing this, but the least trustworthy is learning about a "hot stock" via the media! As a novice, keep in mind that if you hear about a promising idea, its value has most likely already been included in the market. Use money you can afford to lose if you decide to make an investment based on news from the media.

How can I choose equities that will appreciate in value?

Use a broker that enables copy trading to mimic savvy investors automatically.

Investigate based on the criteria that knowledgeable investors use, and then begin analyzing stock data on your own.

Start by taking a look at this advice given by investing master Warren Buffett. "Bought a wonderful company at a fair price is far better than bought a fair company at a wonderful price," he declared.

This is due to the fact that a superb company is more likely to see a spike in value in the future than a fair company, which has little probability of doing so. A further lesson to be learned from Buffett's words is to take your time in locating the true diamonds. Avoid wasting your time on businesses that are "sort of OK." so it's likely that they'll only ever perform "kind of OK."

Buffett has said that you shouldn't buy a stock for ten minutes if you can't see yourself keeping it for ten years. For those of us who need to produce a lot of money right now, that is awful news! However, he is emphasizing the need to maintain discipline.

You won't panic and sell your stocks at the wrong time if you plan to hold them for a long time. Investors who allow their emotions to get the better of them are more likely to sell at a discount or begin purchasing at a premium; if you continue doing this, your portfolio will eventually collapse.

Benjamin Graham, Buffett's mentor, influenced his thinking in many ways.

His well-known book, The Intelligent Investor, was written by him. This presents the concept of "value investing," which entails identifying businesses that are both profitable and trading at a discount to their anticipated future earnings.

Another authority on long-term growth is the seasoned investor Philip Fisher, who is frequently referred to as the "father of growth stocks." Fisher was the owner of Fisher & Company, a very prosperous investment firm, from the 1930s to the end of the 20th century.

Creating Income From Dividends

Novice investors frequently believe that "it takes money to make money." You don't need a lot of money to make money, but it would be lovely to throw a few million dollars into a high-yield investing account and call it a day. All you have to do is start doing whatever it is that you can.

This could mean that some people only need to start with $50. This is undoubtedly preferable to nothing. Naturally, it could feel as though it will take you a lifetime to accomplish your objectives. On the other hand, if you give it some thought, progress can be made quite quickly.

Turning dividends into income is one of the keys to long-term financial success.

One common error made by investors is to take out all of their dividends at the conclusion of each month. Thus, if they put in $100, they withdraw their profits and put that same $100 back in. Although this isn't a bad notion, the truth is that you can't increase your capital in that manner. In fact, to raise your dividends, you would have to make another sizable payment.

Thus, how can you help?

The power of compounding holds the solution. This is the well-known tactic that Warren Buffet allegedly employs.

You need a high-yield account that will pay interest on your account balance as frequently as feasible in order for this to work. Certain accounts with high-interest rates profit from interest on a monthly basis. The high rollers might create accounts that regularly earn interest. However, let's pretend you have monthly capitalizations for the purposes of this book.

Possessing monthly capitalization on your account balance positions you for future large profits. Your gains might not seem like much at first, but as your balance increases, you'll start to reap the rewards of your hard work.

The key in this situation is to keep making your interest payments. Actually, all you have to do is carry over both your initial investment and the money it brings in. The more contributions you are able to make, the faster your dividends will grow.

Think about this instance.

You make a $100 initial contribution. This settles your balance by 1% each month. Following the initial month, you pay $101. Thus, you roll over the $1 in interest rather than taking it out. The interest payment is now computed to be more than $101. You would then receive $102.10 at the end of the second month. You would have $103.02 by the end of the third month, and so forth. To keep things simple, we've utilized a very small quantity. But if you project that over a five-year period, with monthly contributions of $10, you would have $721. You would have $700 if you had just saved the first $100 and an additional $10 per month. This indicates that during a five-year period, you will essentially have a 21% rate of return.

Nothing can outspend that. The stock is far from it. You would anticipate making about 5% on your portfolio in a good year. It is unlikely, though, that the stock market will yield a steady 5% annual return for you. There will be good years and difficult years. Let us say, however, that over the course of five years, you do receive a steady 5% return. Over those five years, that would translate into a 25% return rate for you. However, you would miss out on the lifetime compound interest benefit.

For this reason, over time, the power of compound interest can assist you in becoming both an investor and a saver. Its amazing feature is that you don't need a sizable initial investment. All you have to do is roll over what you have to start.

When you get to retirement, you might use the same amount of money to cover your costs once your capital has significantly rolled over. Everyone's main worry, after all, is what to do when their time on earth comes to an end and they are unable to work. Because of this, when it comes time for you to retire,

Your investment ought to be able to provide you with a respectable amount of money at this stage, enough to help you fund your retirement. In this sense, you will require less money when you retire, and your lifestyle will be simpler. This is an important thing to think about since the more ostentatious your lifestyle gets, the more money you will need to support it.

However, this does not imply that you have to become penniless and subsist on leftovers. It does, however, indicate that you should exercise caution in where you spend your money. In the end, you will have more money if you start investing sooner. It's this that can help you live the kind of life you desire.

People only take out the interest that this kind of account produces each month when they retire. What it does is let you maintain your principal—the entire amount invested—while it keeps giving you dividends every month. This is an investment that, when you stop to think about it, you can pretty much put up and forget about. If not, you would constantly be tempted to spend your savings whenever you felt like it. Indeed, crises do occur. But you'll be able to watch your nest egg grow as long as you don't touch those savings.

IDEAL's "E" stands for Expenses. Generally speaking, when it comes to your investment property, property-related expenses are deductible. You cover the mortgage, insurance, utilities, and interest. All costs incurred by a property manager, as well as those related to maintenance and improvement projects, are write-offs. Investing in real estate entails numerous costs and obligations. For the benefit of landowners investing in real estate, all expenses can be written off under current tax legislation. If you incur a loss on an investment property or business—whether through a loss you took on purpose or not—you can deduct that expense from your income taxes for a number of years. This is a very technical and aggressive approach that some individuals might enjoy. It's yet another advantage of real estate investing.

A - Gratitude

In IDEAL, the letter "A" represents admiration. The value growth of the underlying investment is known as appreciation. We invest for this purpose, among others. Additionally, it can increase our net worth. Even though many San Francisco homes today are valued at several million dollars, in the 1960s, the same property was likely only worth a car's worth, if not less. Since the neighborhood has grown in popularity over time, there has been an exponential increase in real estate values compared to 20 years ago due to the increased demand for it. Those who were able to witness it or were in the right place at the right time have had a 1000-fold rise in their investment returns as a result. That's gratitude. The finest investment you can make without incurring a lot of risk is this one. The finest thing is real estate for investment. Throughout the duration of your ownership, someone is paying you to live in the home, pay off your mortgage, and generate revenue (positive cash flow).

L: Leverage

The term "other people's money" is often used to describe the leverage represented by the letter "L" in IDEAL. This is what happens when you spend a tiny portion of your money on a more expensive item. This works as a kind of leverage for your down payment, giving you ownership over an item that you couldn't otherwise purchase without the loan. Compared to the stock market, where leverage is mostly used for options trading or "on Margin" purchases, real estate leverage is more common and less dangerous. Leverage is frequently used in real estate. If they did not have all the money needed to purchase real estate, they would not do so. Over 33% of transactions are conducted entirely with cash as we continue to recover. Still, around two-thirds of all transactions include funding of some kind. This implies that when it comes time to make a real estate investment, the vast majority of buyers on the market have access to the leverage potential.

A real estate investor would utilize a mortgage to leverage the remaining 90% of the purchase price if they intended to buy a $100,000 home with a 10% down payment. Assume for the moment that the local market grows by 20% the following year. At this point, the real estate is worth $120,000. Leverage-wise, the property's value increased by 20%. With this 20% increase in property value, the investor's return on investment has quadrupled compared to their $10,000 down payment. Also called return on cash for cash. This is 200% since a $20,000 increase in the entire value is now due and payable on the $10,000 down payment.

Although leverage has its advantages, it is not always beneficial. During the nadir of the real estate market in 2007, many investors were overly reliant on leverage. They were unable to withstand the downturn of the economy. You can ensure the stability of your investments and your capacity to hold onto and settle debt. The historical data indicates that there will probably be more booms than busts in the future. But we have to keep going forward. In any market we are in, we will not be defeated by the adverse effects if we plan and prepare more while increasing our net worth.

Real estate investing is much more than just cash flow and appreciation, despite the misconception held by many. As we've already indicated, you can benefit much from each real estate investment property. Making the most of each investment's potential rewards is crucial.

It can also serve as a guide for you while buying any type of investment property you may choose. Every piece of real estate you purchase ought to adhere to the acronym IDEAL. Should the underlying property fail to meet all requirements, there ought to be a rationale. Generally speaking, if an investment doesn't fit the rules, you should PASS.

Consider, for example, a story I own about a home I purchased early in my real estate profession. It remains my biggest investing blunder to date. This is a result of my failure to adhere to the IDEAL principles that you are now studying. I still had very little experience, and I was really innocent. In a gated community, I purchased an empty lot. The land already had a homeowners association (HOA; a monthly charge) because of its lovely features and the possibility of more homes being developed there. The property's potential for future appreciation was highly anticipated, but the market crashed, and the Great Recession, which lasted from 2007 to 2012, began. Which sections of the IDEAL guidelines have I missed? Do you know?

First, let's talk about "I". There was no revenue from the empty lot. Sometimes, this is acceptable, particularly if the deal is too good to pass up. Although not particularly good, this price was a good place to start. To be honest, I thought about advertising a camping area on Craigslist or selling the trees on the empty lot to the nearby mill in order to generate some cash. However, there are better locations to camp, and the lumber isn't valuable enough. Because of my expectations, I was unable to respond to reasonable and logical inquiries. Therefore, I didn't really pay attention to income. I paid dearly for my hubris. Since land cannot be depreciated, this investment did not profit from depreciation. Following the IDEAL real estate investing guideline, we are currently at zero for two. All I can do is hope the land gains value to the point where it can be sold. Let's just refer to it as a costly lesson. You will also receive these "learning lessons"; attempt to steer clear of them all.